S. A. Mulder

No Ordinary Time

S. A. Mulder

DEDICATION

How do you even begin to dedicate something that has taken the support and kindness of so many people? To those of you whose love resides deep in my heart-my gratitude has no bounds. To those of you whose friendship has urged me on to live within this called obedience-the gift of that support is more than I deserve. To those who made space for me at the table to learn to my fill-you opened a door once tightly locked and made it possible to see what it means to know something so completely.

CONTENTS

No Ordinary Time

Under the Catalpa Tree

I see it there
and know full well
its cycled presence
through daily passing.

Its wide green expanse
a guardian canopy.
Thinking I'd like to lay out
under the catalpa tree,

In the purple shade
of its umbrella leaves—
watch the orchid
blossoms fall.

Feel them land light
on my skin
like remembered whispers
from promised days,

to be still; as layer
on layer of weightless petal
hide me from view
and every breath becomes

their heady, fetid
perfume as vision blurs
with creamy mouths
and spotted throats.

To lie, still, to wait
as the days count out
and blossoms rot,
with me, together-

weep into the earth,
ears filling. Silent,
breath escaping
with my spirit

to float as a universe
of pollen flees in the early
summer wind
to fly far, and far away.

Fooled

I roll over   pull the heat of your leaving
back up to my chin, breathing
in the pillow warmth of last night   in order
to ease waking to a day   that is more of the same.

Stretching into a morning communion   of hot coffee,
toast with grapefruit jam.   The bitter, the sweet forced down
along with the fast cooling flavor of earth.

Today will be a good day.   Sun has overcome
darkness creeping across the edges of trees   and window.
Frost paints the railing.   Funny how light makes us fools
to forget the coldness of morning, but fool even more for stepping

through the door onto its shard sharp iciness.   Piercing feet
to bone but less so for looking full   face to the sun
feeling its penetrating heat melt away the scales from my eyes.

Dawn begins its rush to disappear   rising up from where it lay
lifting to the air as a wisp   dripping from pin prick sharp holly leaves.
With one last lung filling drag on the crystal shot morning
holding it deep in until it begins to thaw.

Keeping it there a reminder   as I go back,
crossing the threshold from sacred to profane
to be fooled again tomorrow.

Night Walk

              we traipsed he and i across
                  the vaporous arch
        gray velvet against onyx   murmuring
                  to ourselves   contemplations
                      of the irrational night
                                  mind-
                  in his were held eons
        paced, in mine turnings.
                          too soon descent-
                                  separation keenly felt save
              the burning
                  memory of light

Clockwork Crown

When you look do you hear it?
From behind my placid, half
lidded eyes-

the frenetic construction of
work left undone roiling behind
a flattened smile?

A sinew deep ache
craving deliverance from
this place I am

        --this whitewashed soul
covered over and shot through
with broken starlight and earthy clay.

My eyes close
tight against the call
as my hands fly

with all the unspoken worlds
flinging them into cobbled orbits,
a dervish reel, reordering,

composing a tinkling concerto
to the heavens of letter
line   riot   ruin.

When, at last, they fall in rest
at my sides once more -- words
and worlds spin their progresses

                --a clockwork crown
hovering above my brow.

Dirty Dishes

Your voice whispers
in folded laundry   a benediction
love song   tiny hands clap in their hidden tune.
Communion poured out in sippy cups,   a graham cracker
Eucharist dissolving in milk.   I am now a missionary
to the supermarket, where peace is found and offered
amidst the canned goods   given to
tired strangers in the checkout line.

Sabbath found not in altars and pews but moments
and breaths   in pre-sleep arms wrapped slack
around my neck a holy embrace   hot coffee poured before
the waking hour approaches.   You dwell in the between
amongst.   I meet you when I can   you wait for me
no less   making the meeting sweet, but always it's
the unexpected place daily   I find your help and
dirty dishes.

Violet Sky

Whirling dervishes of Autumn
still but desperate
for the twirl, toss and sway,
fling their arms,
unthreading their sleeves to the wind.

Season's turn, ripe as it is
shows frost in the clouds;
proof the snows will come.
Too soon.
Days shortened,

bring the dreaming's end.
There are no fairy tales
writ to stave away the cold,
warm the waning spirit with hopes
afresh, or delight.

That spring has past, summer
at a loss-
the ruddy golds of fall flee
into the violet sky where dreams
and heroes of the long night go.

Then

I feel most free when their eyes are averted, mouths covered with hands.

Then can I stretch my truth out to the sky, knowing it cannot be swallowed,

will not be taken or looked on with pity and fear.
I can release it to the clouds to be pulled

from the depths of hidden and borne away.
Then. Then.

Will I walk in freedom I will pass to look deep into eyes forced open, to see

and listen for the creaking silence of those with nothing left to say.

Handiwork

fingers twitch with phantom
work, worrying the air
--the way a dying soul
picks at the edges of its
death bed
eyes scanning
~~avoiding~~
as if the seeing would -dangerously-
reignite the lingering,
suffocating embers.

inhale.
still.
wait,

until you learn to let go.

The Stand

Grounded I stand   whole
so full of the living as I feel
roots split my heels   burrow deep
into the earth.

Arms lift to the open air,
fingers aching   stretching
reaching as far as they can until

at last sun piercing their tips brings forth
first green, then rose, then white   fragrant branches
pulsing with life   effervescent
joy exploding in a hundred different directions.

Fixed I begin   the watch knowing what
is to come.   I will see them
arrive, go about their own living.
I will shade them cool in heavy heat,
hold them in my branches as they build
their tiny castles in the sky.   Arms will reach
and span   each embrace   life again

I will know there is no sadness
in the autumn sun   as I use to feel.   Those last fragments
of warmth go deep   igniting the core in preparation

11

for the coming cold
whispering *He is here* through every ring,
each branch.   Leaves may fall and scatter;
merely weaknesses,   failures of a past life that held
low hope, all let go.   In my watching I will see them
            carry my love out
on that long, long day.   Many will say how good it all was,
too late for it to matter.   He will know me there and will come
to greet   before his own roots begin.

The years will flow;   rest in the winter with one eye the guard.
Rising with spring sap running like rapids over smooth
stones   awakening buds full to promises day.
When the time comes I will go

leaving behind wisdom reaching to the heavens, and
love.   There will be joy, layered deep
for having nourished the air life breathed, witnessing the generations
left behind   saplings of a future   nurtured
from the stand. This past forgotten but stretching on
unbeknownst in the midst, evident none the less.

On Meeting Faith

Oh! There you are. That self
reserved   for those
willing to see the rancorous and wild   lying
along side the tender, bruised soul of His beloved.

Neither here,   nor there.   Yet filled
with the promise of rising, just outside
the waging.   We cross and each
stumble the perilous path chosen for us.

Unprepared   to brush against
what is already prepared. Unprepared
to receive   our prophesy ringed in jagged edges.
Though it pains us

to carry it   it bloodies the unsuspecting and
those who thought they knew a better way.
We each bear our paths. Though many choices appear
before   us.

There is but one for me,
for you.
So, let me consecrate this you
this set apart   you.

In the name of the Father
may their
stones fall impotent
at your feet.

In the name of the Son may
you rise
brilliant pierced
and whole.

In the name of the Holy Spirit
may you blaze.
This journey made
for you only

and though the other sees
through cataracted lens
He sees you.
I see you.

May we each learn well
to walk the rebellious   beautiful
way He has entrusted
us to go.

Amen.

Passing Through

Is there a way to shuck the soul   as a husk,
lift off the heart the cumbersome
          weight
of existence?

To then congress freely through air &
light, to pass   complete   through another leaving
          behind
only the hint of a scent,   tenderness to trace
their own broken   soul with a memory
of life?

Were I to rend   each depleted layer   untended
by care   would what remains
          remain
enough to go upward   or out or, more likely,
become the faintest puff dispersed   silk
and ashen leavings   a spiral heartbeat on the current
          scattering unremarked?

Scoured

I broke
every window
wide.

Letting snow
pile in
with the wind.

Scoured
my soul
raw

In the living
room.
Leaving

the
rags
behind.

Inheritance

I want to wear the softness of you
on my memory
inhale the uncorrupted sweetness
of your hours old breath

pulling you into my lungs;
brush the lanugo on your shoulders and store
the feeling of it in my fingertips,
for always.

I need to carry the nearness of my tears.
To remain held in this moment
as I stroke the shell curl of your ear hardly
bigger than the end of my thumb

To see you stretch new strength with shaky
determination
and know the echo of your first bursting
                    wail will fill the air for generations.

Holy Yes

Creation explodes in an unseen riot of existence,
        each particle
            brings praise in its doing,
in its joyful, mutinous rebellion
            of death.

Green, its very 'ness'
        the Paraclete of this hidden realm,
            extols the prophecy of
            fearless life.

Each cell exhales truth
while veins pulse their purpose.

Until-
at last-
in that reconciled season,
all falls to the earth.

To feed,
        again,
            this answer,
                that only proves the question,
                    with a holy yes.

No Greet

There is no greet
in this day.

The sun has wrapped himself in the clouds,
refusing to wake.

My heart drags itself from sleep,
reluctant to begin this yesterday's coffee morning.

Words mumble and shift,
Their truths no more than hollow ringing in my ears.

The wind, desperate for the sky, bellows
to the clouds   Depart!

With one great heave,
the despondent sky turns and hides itself deeper in its blanket of gray.

The microwave beeps, coffee hot, again
and there it is.

A single bird-ignorant of the storm   ratchets up his call
in defiance of the bluster.

A guileless caroler daring the sky to drown his song.
Searching the trees, I find no evidence

No breast or feather-
only notes flying to the hidden sky.

He knows for Whom he sings.
without regard for the world's dictatum,

He does so anyway.
Perhaps, this is all the truth I need.

Today.

Threadbare Cloth

Reading the cold face,
   like Braille,
      searching for recognition
         in the lines.

I believe in God the Father.

The empty eyes,
   emblematic of an
      empathetic truth?

Creator of heaven and Earth.

Bronze relief conveys
   no peace
      to this twisting soul.

And in Jesus Christ, his only begotten son.

I am begat from threadbare cloth.
    Frayed.
    Torn.
    Transparent.
Broken in its wholeness.
    Weak in the warp.

He was crucified, died, and was buried.

A remnant, this shred.
    No solid bronze,
    for eternity to wear.

On the third day.

Convenient Glow

We half-watch our way through
believing we are in possession

all the while rushing through the long,
slow telling. We turn our backs

to the vastness, dark, hovering
around some convenient glow like

moths destined to crash ourselves against
the light and die with every blow.

Enough

Where goes the strength of stride when time bends
the spine to its fetal return, of sorts.

The world misted cataracted gray and soft. A palsied
stroke replacing a confident caress.

Will you rouse to my whisper, breath catch
at its thought? Will enough of me remain

when the glass is unkind and the blood memory of flesh
exhausts itself? Will we close our eyes together

forehead to forehead breathe in, I you
and you I, before the agonal sigh?

Ushering

The look of Winter deceives.
Beneath its surface warmth
energy, growth   foments-
each heartbeat ripe,
humus rich;   within

brittle branches
where the catkin begins to creep,
long before we know it's there,
or that first heating of a spring sunrise
lifts dew from bud.   Winter,

on first glance looks gray
depleted; an end.   Don't be fooled-
it is an ushering. Fulfillment.

Renewal arrives in various forms;
the driest,
        coldest,
                weariest ends
bring about a most glorious   rebirth.

Take Note

Take note of this.
And take it in your stride.
This day in day out is little more than that.
Darkness may only be darkness and light,
light the burden
of thinking otherwise slows the
mind burdens the step impedes
the vision so that what you see is never what
is right there, right here
reaching behind or beyond overfills
your hands leaving you starving for
your hands are never filled with now.

Ghosts

There is within a longing
for the deepest hours.

Ones where entire days
disappear in a blink

where worlds are discovered,
word by word.

Those simmering moments when day paints the hall
with shafts of ambered gold,

and dust swirls a riotous ballet
through light while in the silence

echoes of childish squeals are held
as ghosts skip airlessly by.

Timeless

Shall I meet you in shadowed cold?
Beneath the low-slung branches

-of the old pine-

heavy with snow.

The one which has stood in the corner
since before the first dwelling was built.

We can crawl under
-speak our dreams into the needles-

to be exhaled in the uppermost branches
-into the ear of God.

Hide there

-apart from time-

and linger

or love.

We are whole there.
Timeless.
Always.

Her Lot

Hers is a different lot
no current rolling soft
to carry care.

Ripples here are pavement hard,
they trip you up,
        skin you raw.

The best hoped
is a path of crush-
but never the yielding of grass
for this wildling way.

Is there a poetry of concrete,
an aria for ramshackle
        and broke?

Hers is a poetry dry,
        fistfuls-
mouthfuls of sand and dust.
No honeyed liquid
verse to soothe-

it comes in puffs and gags
        if it comes at all.

Pockets

In the beginning

    did He know?
Did He know that I would walk the very edge
fill my vision on every side with trees, air full
with the cinnamon scent of pine straw crushed
by feet and crystals of sky,
and water   on the verge of ice deep fast?

God created

    did He Know?
Did He know earth would overflow overfill
my eyes, bones overwhelm, and hurt full
weight like stones worn
smooth from use, pain would press
and stretch   and follow?

Heaven and earth

    did He know?
Edges blurring one into another as I walked
to the very edge   rocks upon rocks heavy in every
pocket   where ice met flow

        waiting to step.

Granite Call

He asked,
        "How would you live your last day-
if you knew it to be so?"

        "Easy," I replied.

"I would walk out into the cold air-
in my shirt sleeves,
face to the sun.
I would watch its light stream through
each, singular branch,
feel its tireless warmth
touch my lips."

breath

"I would listen
deep into the veins of trees
for that eternity song pulsing,
and hear the crash of my footsteps echo
an uneven heartbeat."

breath

"I would open my palms to the birds
and they would land.
Unafraid.
For they know I now understand their truth."

breath

"I would bathe in frost,
drip dry on the rise
and wait.
Cleansed.
Naked."

breath

"I would close my eyes
to see the mountains.
...to hear their granite call--
and open them to find myself there."

Sheaving

There are no more rumors,
of war,
just only and is.

Hollow icons.
Standing.
Mouthpieces of broken air.

Nodding chaff
waving their approval,
applaud.

"Yes!", they say. "Of course."
"That was what we meant all along."
they rasp in their cultivated lines.

Suffering
only mild confusion,
when the wind changes,
shifting their gaze where

refreshed,
they may begin again-
their hissing applause
to the burning sky.

There is no dissent
until the sheaving begins.
And then, too late,
the swath is cut.

The leavings lament...
"If only the wind
had changed again,
we might have seen this coming."

Rived

Why
echoes across the land,
old as stone;
hollow in the gut.

The rived soul gapes
                howls,
and is carried-
  -emptied-

    like ash on the wind
to every corner.
From the deepest valley
to highest peak filling the shuddering air

    shattering the heavens
    scattering shards
    to pierce the hearts
    of the unhearing-

    stop the blathering mouths
    of the useless speakers.

Until all that remains
is desolate.

Purged.
Laid out,
scorched, and raw.

Only then

will there tread souls
who both heard the wretched victims
and move to cover,
comfort--

--with weeping hands to touch;

and gather the splinters
of broken heaven
pushing them deep
into the blackened earth
   and rise again
to rise   in brilliant green;
      new.

The Empty Place

The small rupture of a soul
its sundered spark drifting away,
a wild cherry leaf
        falling in empty air.

once separated, not returned.
the charter removed, a single
        future
both return and loss.

some things you
don't come back from,
only grow different
        in the empty place.

Rise

        cast me as ash
           like fallen snow

        to float
        the four ways
                     and light
        soft
        on currents

        to the clouds.

        to fall
           to rise
         and rise
      and rise.

Virginia's Reel

She struggled along in
her slow, halting gait
I could see
each pant of breath in the falling air
as she whispered,
"James Dean should never sing
children's songs"
and giggled.

Stopping, she ceded permission
to the detritus
as cellophane wrapper's whorled
a riotous Virginia Reel
around her patchwork feet

quietly she sang,
"Nearer my God to thee.
Nearer to thee".

Kitten

Demitasse polka dots-
all satin, slip, and shine.
The echo of its feel
    in my fingertips,
though forbidden to touch.

The voluminous, shushing crinoline
admonishing me to not betray

this tiny infringement
on her memories.
Because, after all, they were hers.
not mine.

Kitten heels.
She use to call me kitten.

I always sat outside her memories,
care, and kindnesses;
those were reserved for the ones
revolving in her orbit.

Fresh washed and "darling",
air kisses   tinkling ice
sun dripping smiles
peered through baluster veil.

But still she called me kitten.

Morning Hour

Rising.
　　arching my back,
inhaling the cool, gray light
　　　　I inspect the day.

Rain has washed night away,
　　tipping pine needles
and tiny leaflets
　　　　with infant sparks.

Walking in the barely light,
　　I anticipate coffee,
soothing words from
　　　　ancient pages.

Cup in hand,
　　I pull open the heavy glass door,
dividing in from out,
　　　　welcome the world's
　　　　weightless chill,

Silence of trees that is not quiet,
   and the rolling hum
from distant pavement.

Lighting candles while
   waiting coffee cools, I search
the sunrise for prophecy,
      imploring the chorusing birds

their joy
   questioning the wind
it's ceaseless praise.
      As my heart beats out prayers
            words won't touch.

Unquiet

I have become,
                  unquiet.

Though utter nothing.

Were you to look in my mouth
you would see
words I did not say
engraved on my tongue.

The ones that tell
of who I am,
where I am come.

You would read myriad dreams,
unmanifest,
aborted.
Abundant.

You would read tomes
and volumes
of what I have seen,
                  not said.

You would discover
broken poetry,
pithy retorts,
wisdom's words earned
but undelivered.

For every word
you would learn
the light behind my eyes.

Why I wear resignation
-a tattered garment-
as a cloak.

You would find plumbed darkness,
ocean deep and equally chill.
broad expanses of green and sky,
    warm.

You see,
you go on without thought,
granted, without malice,
about the weather,

stocks,
the state of things according
to your safe distance,
using indifference as punctuation.

Periods,
prudently placed,
to dispel contradictions.
To leave uninvited
doubt and different.

Yes, in silence,
there is delight
in the unquiet.
While you live your one,
highly punctuated life,

I live thousands.

Marking the days-
-in ordinary time.

Piled paper ornaments.
Congratulating the small,
celebrating the not so

ordinary.

A chorus of off-key voices,
whose years don't all add up to ten
rivaling a tabernacle of perfection
in the breathy joy of it all.

No ordinary time.

Piercing cold rises up my bared body,
looking west.
Puffs of air define empty space.
Gooseflesh declares the living
a full shiver of life.

There is no ordinary time.

A welling, a rising.
This tidal embrace-
lines dissolving in darkness-
breathless.

Response.

A welling, a rising.
This tidal call-
where lines of each are blurred into one.
Breathless.
Until there are two.

There is no ordinary time.

Each breathing moment
in
    out
in
    out
in
    out
until slowed, stopped.

Marking the days-
There is weeping.

Rejoicing.

Mundacity and riot.
Simplicity and the wildly
orchestrated dance.

Ordinary?

In.

    Out.

In.

    Out

In.

    Out.

There is no ordinary time.

Nona

The smell of her palm
is onions
and bread. Then honey.

With each breath,
I draw in the scent of a thousand meals
reimagining the delicate sounds of silver and glass.
Conversations lost; arguments edged with smiles.

In her palm I feel the very bringing in,
a harvest of time.
A cry of new life.
The blessing of smoothed hair,

a consolation of care.
A reprimand deserved, from obligation bestowed;
out of love, regretted.

From that palm,
I feel gladness and sorrows back through generations.
Hear scattered stories,
whispered secrets.

There are also oranges.
And sweet milk coffee in jadeite cups.

I breathe her in.
Breathe in that which marks who she is.
I breathe in for all I am worth,
thinking that if I could just inhale her

she would go on forever.

Vows for an Anniversary

When time bends the fingers strange
slows the rampant mind,
and dandelions reflect the universe,
a delicate parable,
of kind.

When gait and amble
hitch and sway,
this ghost will still remember
the running

    spent...

the play.

Touch,
and taste,
and breath,
and line:
what you laid out
before me
I've greedily kept as mine.

When you've dissolved before my eyes,
and flesh leaves bone,
sinew dies-
we'll meet, we vapors

    floating

as ancient lovers,
rise.

Together
we will drift

    entwine

Till every wisp and atom
of me is you,
every minim of you
is mine.

Stone Song

would that you could grind
your fist through the viscera of
my flesh
-breach this weakened heart.
you would still not there echo
the recoiling sting
of that which I wish
I had not known.
and I am weary
of teaching stones to sing.

Shivaree

The air is bracing, welcomed into
a door opened just enough for him to enter
with all his early morning energies.

Today he brings green, the fragrance of grass,
leaf, and new   something sweet, too,
but undefined.

He stirs up the brown of toast and coffee
mingling it all morning fresh.

Hospitality granted, he goes about the room
making work of waking up the tired corners,
conversing with the blinds.

His busy-ness unhurried, thorough.
I sip my coffee not ignoring my guest
only leaving him to his
new found companions.

Outside the door it has begun. The trees leaning in
careful of their tender growth, to listen.

It's the morning Shivaree!

From every corner it comes; delicate trills, racing scales,
off key kaks, come hither whistles,
chips and giggles-
an avian cantillation
rising from the wood

up through morning, transforming to the song of day.
Air, weary of his internal pleasantries, slips out
with a stir of nightgown
to beg branches applaud the goings on.

Clouds dip low to eavesdrop as sun lifts her heavy head
in warming encouragement   each own bringing its offering
to the discordant harmony,

this teeming, this mass of gratitude.
This holy Shivaree.

Prism

A feather weight of lurid colors
graze hand lines deepened with time and hard use.
Fill and fade
transforming the dry,
the hardened,
to mirth.
A memory made of youthful delight.
The delicate tracing, tickling, tinkling,
sparkling
fading themselves.
The light drifts,
callously moving away.
Stealing away the playful.
Robbing the lightness.
Stilling.
Stalling.
Gone.

To the Table

Come to the table. Oh, love
there is room for you and all is made
ready. Come.

To the table, oh, love
bring your tears for there are hearts
enough gathered to bear
your ache.

Oh, love, bring your joy
for there are hearts
enough gathered
to toast in celebration.

Come to the table. Oh, love
we are gathered a broken contingent
with hearts enough to welcome
you in. Come.

To the table, oh, love
for here we sup
with compassion,
hungered for peace.

We drink with mirth,
our cups overflowing
with hope, weep in the quiet
moments, embrace.

Come to the table, oh, love
for all is prepared and we have
a place made ready
for you.

Fugitive Dreams

Rummaging through corners of memory,
searching-
hoping to find that word.
The original phrase-the key
to loose all the world's locked away.

I find no key.
No hidden wonderland door,
or potion,
to expose my fugitive dreams.

Only stillness.
Only make the coffee,
then the bed,   ordinary stillness.

And windows.
Whose dusted panes filter
the brightness of out.

The spiral chase of life
in that too bright
that causes me to squint
and cover my ears.

I search again for a remembered
garden I have never seen.
To walk its hillocks,
brush each sweet pea, rose, and lilac with my mind,

feel the cool damp of the dark earth,
bare footed and overalled.
Overwhelmed by the fragrant fecundity of living.
And green.

It is all so vivid,
this unvisited place,
that my fingers tingle with the velvety prickle of each leaf and
stalk
-ears ring with echoes of phantom jay and rook.

The last lurch of coffee brews,
the dryer hums,
and I sit-
back turned to the window.
Longing for a place I've never been.

Of a Sunday

What steady plod leads to this?
Are you there hidden,
sepulchered
behind a veil of our own re-creation?

We shuffle together
in Sisyphean pilgrimage-
        habitual markers-
mired in amber piety;

hands clasped,
politely, in lap,
nodding our corporate assent,
giving and taking our peace.

Eyes forever washing corners
and rafters for hints of light.
Desperate for escape,
to shatter the Sunday face and loose its hold.

For once shoved,
        -with benediction-
out the door,
Finally freed to wander,
to worship.

To laugh with you,
wipe tears away.

kiss the wild, wild face
of your creation each night

drink it in new
and rich
each dawn.

To chase you,
find you,
never losing sight.
To weep
or mourn,
hands firmly in yours.

To rail in your hall,
accuse and curse
out in the open
yet never leave your side-

Is it strange
others miss you
through the week?
Solace found only at Sunday's break,

Or odd to find you sequestered
in the mismatched cathedral
of this wide, wide world
save for an hour or so
        of a day?

Hum

The low hum hovers, semi quiet
while a gray spring of fog and old leaves

carries on beyond the glass.
A noiseless chorus of daily life

in an empty house. The surface of a drink pulses
with a subterranean heartbeat,

an invisible rhythm tapping out wavelengths in the quiet.
Breath is an intrusion, the shift of sheets

a monumental rift   creating an uproar.
Dust motes disarrayed of their silent

dance by the irreverent disruption.   A moment later
their mindless wanderings restored,

   as though never disturbed.

Damp Dark

...whose courses,
for millennia,
   were meant to rise.
Choose instead, now,
to fall.

The beckoning of loam
superior to the open sky?
This damp dark.
Quiet.

Stilling the flight.
The stalling of the constant
Struggle of current.
Expedient.

This rest.
No word filled exhaustions,
No mumbling oaths
Or falsity of brow.

The fall
This fall.
Is far superior
To the reluctance of now.

Evensong for Friday

Words, garbled and tuneless,
break free.

With shining eyes and dimples.
arms flung wide,

a crooked and wobbly gait.

No requiems here,
only offerings of light.

Off key joy effervesces,
radiant and overflowing.

Tiny hands build towers to the gods.

Singing brilliant praises to the air,
only the angels can define.

Kyrie

So much life, mine own,
has been about erasure.

Never there.

A yearbook casually dropped in an autumn fire,
old photographs, brittle, ignite
like fireflies on the updraft.

Never there.

Lord, have mercy.

Negatives from another era curling,
twisting, blackening, melting
a bone deep desire to disappear.

Never there.

Christ, have mercy.

Ash as proof of life.
Scattered, swept,
Removed.

Never there.

Lord, have mercy.

Wild Wood

I have no use for wooden soldiers
marching in their scripted grooves
nor crafted words,
your god.

I choose the wild
wood, gnarled growth
a knotted soul
with which to build.

Give me aged,
broken, branches liberated
bark loosed, fecund,
all the world

displayed in leaf rust,
its drift and swirl,
a reckoning with the air.
that I may breathe

its composted fragrance
ripe rich
shot through with time.
let rot, decay remind.

No, not your god for me
nor endless groove
while Trojan soldiers, these,
return to dust, foretold.

between

it is the late breaking morning
that isn't, when night overstays
its welcome.

in this not day dark
memories walk more tangible
than ghosts

more terrifying for their reality.
awake, the reluctant real true
meets consolation turned confusion.

pitch melts into the trees,
day arrives and light evaporates
all trace of what was a dream.

Hopeworn

I'm tired of wealthy prophets
    with their elevated platforms;
soft words spoken to move the multitudes,

freedom that speaks emptiness to my truth.

I am bored of the lyrical,
    the beautiful,
        the *right*.
Where is my world in them?

I am sick of politic
    that shifts with the wind,
        of rhetoric and swollen promises;

made to the few,
meant to break the masses.

I am exhausted of this world where love is suspect
    and life a balloted argument.

Wearied by those who speak a prophesied peace
while feasting like ravenous vultures

on those whose real peace
    wears dusty sandals and dirty hands.

This weariness, though,
    is worn out by hope.

One for a world where love is breathed
    into the hollow places-
supped on, filling famished hearts.

One that is written in the sky,
    a tenet of practice laid bare
in blistered hands

with evidence and trace
    of an overflowing
to obliterate a compassionate void.

Baptism Dust

Digging holes
    with my plastic shovel;
clinging to the handle of a tin bucket as if it would
        protect me from the world.

Squatting, small knees bare,
        pixie cut and blue jean shorts,
for what seemed like days.
        Or hours? Minutes?

There was purpose in those holes
        that pulled me so far,
to a quiet space where wild flowers
        grew and dust smelled like all good things.

Little red Keds with scuff proof toes,
        crunched along,
quiet only when I would stoop
        to collect another hole.

It was out there
  He was. Eyes kind.
Upraised open hand, empty of any remembered threat.
  I was unafraid.

And my parents, stock-still by, their misted, mismatched
faces-
  one kind, one blank. Both absent.
There between the three,
  my dusty red Keds.

I go back to that spot, again and again.
  Bucket in hand, rubber soles
grinding the dirt
  with their determined searching.

Never finding the field of holes,
  yet knowing
it will always be there.

Unsuspecting Days

Where do days go
when they disappear unused?
When pain prevails and daylight weighs?

Are they gathered, harvested?
Somewhere wrapped in cotton,
protected, preserved,

waiting to be restored?
Or, do they linger in the periphery,
that they may offer up their unused moments,

to unsuspecting days?
Perhaps they merely drift.
Lost, wasted

a burdened mist,
heavy with the unlived.
Tell me,

where do the days go
when we cannot be there
to live them?

See

You look at my clothes, say
    my soul is ragged.
You look at my skin and tell me
    I've got it all wrong.
You look at my face
    as though it matters.
You look at me and tell me
    If I don't try to fit in,
    I'll never belong.

You look and see only
    what you choose to believe.
See only
    that which is not you,
    only other, no we.
You look and see only
    what you wish it to be.

You see, you don't see,
    in your need to be right
You see, you don't see,
    A soul filled with light.
You see, you don't see.
    A heart that beats strongly.
You see, you don't see,
    He sees us more clearly.

You see, you don't see
    blindness is never just blindness,
    nor only with the eyes.
While one may lack physical vision,
    the sighted see only their lies.

Heat Dream

I breathe in deep,
the dust dry sound
of sandals scraping ground.

The heat-heavy laughter of children-
pushing against the weight of day-
tinkling down around my ankles.

Breathe again
and I am filled with arid browns,
angular greens. Hot coffee too.

Breathe and the smell of bodies grows.
Sweat ripe with living. Sounds; mother calls,
barking dogs, cooking clamor. A splash.

Breathe once more-filling my chest-
the smell of quiet fills with night sounds;
the rasp of a brush through hair, humid yawns.

The hushing sound of a brushed cheek.
One last breath.
I open my eyes and it is gone.

Into

leaning hard,
walking-no, pushing-against the gale;
squinting, face wet.
straining against the is.

silence.

the tumult abruptly stops.
screaming wind shocked into a keening sigh.
straining muscles hitch with surprise;
right themselves.

bewildered stillness.

whence came dissolves to falling snow.
-soundless echoes of what was before
gather at my feet,
erasing old trace.

looking back
dark yawns
it's muffled howl.
a menace veiled in new white.

looking forward-

I step, once-
edgeless white tipping
into the I don't know, unblemished
offering no hint, no line.

each step leads
while marking
where I've been.
I step again.

Just Another Day

Dawn:

light and air, lift,
slip. Seeking, then hiding.
Threads through branches.

Then rushes, shifting
the way a child runs,
arms outstretched, through a field
of wildflowers, leaving a silent wake.

Dawn reaches out to

Day:

Day. Its bright unhiding
disturbs the most. A bold gaze
penetrating, unforgiving.
Demanding,

tasks to be done.
Careers be made. Minutes
expanded into profit.
The 'more' that is never enough.

But dusk.

Dusk:

That falling of day.

It is exhale and gentling,

the quieting.
The flagging sun,

expansive, generous warmth.
Prepares, luxuriously, for rest.
Igniting trees, stroking petal, blade
and leaf alike.

Fondly farewelling while pulling
in the edges of days sprawl.
The Crone of evening presses a finger
to her lips, shushing the light.

Night:

Here begins
the whispering hours.
Velveted footsteps, the settling
and tucking of the day.

Each blossom releases its silent,
fragrant sigh as they close
their petals to the dark.
and day is dismissed to memory.

Here dreams replace the daylight
with her harsh truth. Replacing
it with its own. Until complete
and dawn trips in
anew.

A Poem for 9-4-17

In the quest to be perfect, right,
to be un-human, we become inhumane.

This battle rages in the human heart
festers the human soul. To be above,

gods immortal on earth, ruling shallow kingdoms
taming hearts which beat in syncopated rhythms.

You who would rule donning blinders of right-ness,
obliterate righteousness. Your self-need

to own, profess gold laden half-truths,
grab at the staff of God and rattle it at the world.

Your attempts to breach the cleft of eternity will light
fire to the corpses, reap ash.

Your shanks of gold will farrow only clouds.
Your bully howls will fall silent,

in that eternal second, when the rush of future
explodes the past. What then will be the tillage,

the remain? What harvest
for the silos of memory?

What will victory sound like
in the murmurings of an ashen tongue?

manna

there are gathered moments,
greedily collected around me.
hoarding them
out of fear, grasping them
to stave off the inevitable.

but, like manna gathered
more than can serve,
these days grow bitter and
useless

with the holding.   there is no saving
nor redemption of a day.
it is not in me
to re-create the future

nor re-invent the past
what is   has been.
will not become
any more than it is meant to be

and I am left holding the days,
bitter.   those hours
empty,   which were never mine
to hold.

Dry Bones

Come live old, dry bones   gather
your splinters and fragments   rise

free your dust the wind to lift, swirl
no random trace to course but designed to mark

to fill in gap and break   sketch out the hollow
places taking on form.

Collect old breath   filling the empty
inhale   draw deeply and deeper until

thigh and breast expand   fingertip, vein, and tongue
unroll   tremble and there

each particle, each atom   waits
quivering until at a single touch   the ashen

scatter coalesces   begins new beat & throb while   holy
water falls to quenching.

Now I Lay Me

I could hear them
through the screen.
Late coming July
darkness and heat

filtered their voices,
softened the edges.
I lay between sleep
and awake,

in that strange now
that floats above reality,
staining the ordinary
with shadow,

heightening a hidden sense.
Lulled by Summer exhaustion
and cigarette smoke
sifting in on the breeze

they talked in the past,
always, plans fragmented
like a broken mirror
reflecting only half truths,

while my eyes closed
without me knowing.
I slipped across into night
forgetting I needed to be afraid.

ACKNOWLEDGMENTS

Ghosts and Under the Catalpa Tree first appeared in Barren
Magazine